"There's been a renaissance recently—the church is once again patronizing the arts. It's about time. *Art & Faith* promises to foment a revolution right in your congregation. This book is a highly needed and valuable resource."

Tony Jones, author of *The Sacred Way: Spiritual Practices in Everyday Life* (tonyj.net)

Western Christianity has a problem. It is privately engaging yet publicly irrelevant. Changing the way faith is perceived in the West requires upending the system, not merely tweaking it. Jon Bowles is attempting to do this. . . . Here is a story of a pioneer as well as a pastor.

Mike Metzger, President/Founder of Clapham Institute

Jon Bowles has done us a big favor in writing *Art & Faith*. Historically, art has played an enormous role in communicating the story of Christian faith. But as of late, something has gone wrong. In an Evangelical culture of schlock, trinket, kitsch, cliché and cheap imitation, Jon's book is an important primer and timely reminder of what real art is and the vital role it must play in an authentic expression of faith.

Brian Zahnd, Lead Pastor, Word of Life Church, and author of *Beauty Will Save the World*

ART
&
FAITH

Reclaiming the Artistic Essence of the Church

JON BOWLES

CONTENTS

INTRODUCTION: TWO WORLDS

"This guy is the pastor of the church that meets here."

I knew something made me uncomfortable with the way our current artist introduced me to his close friend, but I was having a hard time putting my finger on it.

It was a bustling First Fridays in Kansas City and our church was still getting used to the thrill of having so many strangers walk in our doors and peruse the art on the walls. First Fridays is a monthly happening in which all the galleries in the Crossroads Arts District open their doors and celebrate local and national talent—it's a festive occasion. Like a party spilling onto the streets, there are pantomime artists on corners, vendors selling food and drinks, fire dancers spewing flames in one parking lot and performance art in another. It's also impossible not to hear music anywhere you go on First Fridays. You absolutely cannot get away from the music. Every block has a band, a musician, a DJ, a guy playing bongos, or two guys playing empty milk crates.

When we first decided to plant our small church in the Arts District, particularly in a quaint gallery space that was available for rent, it seemed like a complete slam dunk. I never hesitated. The prospect of a church that did more than talk about the arts or participate from the fringe was thrilling. I wanted a church that engaged and facilitated the arts in a manner that was relevant to the larger public conversation and community.

In my enthusiasm and naïveté, I was completely unprepared for the two worlds I encountered shortly after moving into our gallery. I realized that reality was perceived by many as split. One cloth, torn in two. Or perhaps differing cloths altogether. If art and faith was the immediate scenery, everyone seemed to be wearing bifocals.

The church world understood locating ourselves in a gallery as a way to reach people. They saw the gallery as a "beach-head for Jesus" and the art itself relatively inconsequential, perhaps only a means to an end. It was assumed our stated mission revolved around "reaching the community."

To this world I struggled to communicate that my goal for us wasn't to *reach* the community. I wanted, rather, to *join* the community. I wanted to join the party. More specifically, I wanted our church to join and participate in the artistic conversation happening all around us because I believe God is there, revealing himself. Besides, it seems right and appropriate that God's people should have a welcomed and constructive voice at the table.

The artistic world, on the other hand, seemingly had no desire to understand the church. (Or maybe they understood us all too well.) They seemed acutely aware of our propensity to reach people and they had no interest in being reached. The woman from whom we rented our gallery took a deep breath as she handed me the keys, "I know you're a church, but please, please try to use this space for something artistic." Her implication being that the two ideas are diametrically opposed.

So here I was on this crazy First Fridays listening to our artist introduce me.

"The pastor of the church that meets here . . ."

"The church . . . that meets here . . ."

You've got it all wrong, I wanted to say. *We don't just meet here—this is us! Our gallery. The church . . . our church . . . my church is hosting your work. We enjoy your art. Speaking as a pastor and curator, I love your work.*

What I actually said was, "Nice to meet you."

The exchange gave me some perspective and sympathy for the young artist. He isn't, after all, a professing Christian and his art certainly isn't what you would typically refer to as "Christian art." It isn't vulgar, by any means, but it also isn't something you would ordinarily see in a church. There are no crosses or doves.

The misunderstanding that night was a matter of perceived roles. The young artist believed our role was one of utility—merely allowing our church *building* to house art. In fact, we are asserting that a church *body* can have an invested, curatorial role in the local art scene. That our space is a gallery, not a building with a steeple, is evidence of a larger truth: we are all artists.

I've slowly and somewhat reluctantly realized that a complete duality has infected the popular imagination. The critical marriage of faith and art has somewhat vanished. The church world is at best dismissive of art, and the art world is, at worst, antagonistic toward the church.

Consider this common exchange heard during First Fridays:

"So, this is a church too? Where do you meet?"

"Right here."

"Here? In the gallery?"

"Yep."

"What do you do with the art?"

Think about it. For many people, works of art need to be taken down in order to worship or talk about God. Something is obviously broken.

I've discovered that redeeming the fragile and shattered relationship between art and faith is largely what Beggars Table is about. Within our local context we want to bring the two worlds together again. Or perhaps more accurately, shed light on the fact that the two worlds are actually one in the same. We want to allow faith to speak to artists in a way that transcends kitsch while also allowing artists to shape our imagination and bring meaning to our faith. Reclaiming the essential role art plays in forming our loves is a driving force behind Beggars Table.

I'm thankful for the opportunity to invite people into this conversation. Hopefully we can take steps toward repairing the damage and reuniting two worlds that were never intended to be estranged. The dream is for the church to once again promote a seamlessness between art and faith that provides meaning for individuals, communities, and the wider world.

1

PICTURE THIS

"Art, from the Lascaux caves to Damien Hirst,
has been always about faith."

—*Makoto Fujimura*

What does it mean to be human? Certainly this is a daunting question with which to begin a book. But to get to the bottom of it, I believe, is to make a case for the reintegration of art and faith. This is a book about how art has formed the imagination of my church toward the kingdom. This book could be about your church too.

The dominant vision of humanity, a vision that dates back to Plato, establishes humankind primarily as a thinking being. In other words, formation and motivation are first and foremost cognitive processes. No one historically claims more credit for the modern cultivation of this vision than René Descartes.

You're probably familiar with the story. In the seventeenth century René Descartes, addressing an existential crisis of doubt and racked with uncertainty, retreats to an isolated room for several days in order to *think* his way through the dilemma. To sum up the story outlined in his book *Discourse on Method* and later in *Meditations,* Descartes realizes that because he thinks—and subsequently doubts—he can find certainty in at least one thing: he exists. Thus the famous maxim, "I think, therefore I am."

Upon this wholly cognitive foundation, Descartes builds a worldview structure that ultimately advocates God's existence. I remember reading *Discourse on Method* for a Western Civilization class in college. I had never heard of René Descartes, and I was moved by his rational argument for God's presence. Submerged in higher education, a kind of hyper-cerebral environ-

By defining belief as "right information" and placing an emphasis on doctrine, it may very well be that the church is operating under an intellectual paradigm and calling it another name.

ment that was unexpectedly threatening to my faith, Descartes' carefully plotted discourse seemed almost hallowed. When I discovered years later that Descartes had actually been commissioned by the church to prove God's existence and thus his whole crisis had a religious agenda, it really wasn't much of a surprise.

Today we live in Descartes' assumptions; the meaning of humanity is understood rationally, that is, our fundamental orientation to the world is through knowledge. This Cartesian model for humanity has been unquestioningly absorbed by the dominant culture for the past several hundred years, yet perhaps no single institution has built itself more aggressively upon this presupposition than the Protestant church.

Because the assumption is that human flourishing—human development and health—is a cognitive process, the modern church tends to foster an overly cerebral account of what it means to be or become a Christian. To be fair, the church rarely claims knowledge as its foundation. We are taught from an early age that faith rests in belief, not intellect; that before we are thinkers, we are believers. This is fine as far as it goes. The problem is belief, as understood inside Protestant practice, is largely a heady business and one that ignores the rest of human experience. By defining belief as "right information" and placing an emphasis on doctrine, it may very well be that the church is operating under an intellectual paradigm and calling it another name, says professor and theologian James K. A. Smith.

> This model of the human person seems just to move the clash of ideas down a level to a clash of beliefs. Those beliefs often still look like the propositions and ideas of the rationalist model . . . The beliefs that orient me still seem quite disconnected from my body and with little or no attachment to the things I do as a body, and so with little attachment to the others that my body bumps into, embraces, hugs, and touches.[1]

The result is what Smith calls a bobblehead Christianity "so fixated on the cognitive that it assumes a picture of human beings that look like bobbleheads: mammoth heads that dwarf an almost nonexistent body."[2] This talking head version of Christianity may boast a foundation of belief over knowledge, but it still provides a jarringly reductionistic account of the human experience. It also makes for a faith that easily comes undone.

Why was the university environment so threatening to my faith? I believe it was, at least partly, because my spiritual formation up to that point was largely built on propositions and ideas. When my religious understanding was challenged with conflicting knowledge, my faith began to crumble. Because I hadn't developed an intuitive and experiential faith, I couldn't draw on my senses for support. At that point I became an all-too-familiar creature—a defensive Christian.

Again, what does it mean to be human? There is a compelling alternative to the longstanding vision of humanity as thinkers. Advocated by such men as Augustine and Jesus Christ himself, this radical vision of humanity asserts that we are—fundamentally and primordially—lovers. To be human, they propose, is chiefly to love. Meaning it is what we love, not merely what we learn, that defines us.

What social scientists are now discovering is that a person's character and virtue are not formed primarily on a cognitive level but rather by those processes happening below his or her level of awareness. It is not the conscious self that drives our behavior, but what we love, unconsciously, that is responsible for most of our actions. We might say in response to Descartes, *I think, but mostly I am.*

"The story is told one level down," says author David Brooks in the introduction to his book *The Social Animal.* The human mind can receive as many as 11 million messages in a given moment; of these, only 40 may be consciously processed. Where instinct and behavior are concerned, we are drawing from the vast depth of the emotional inner mind rather than the analytical outer mind for instruction. That's why, Brooks goes on to suggest, we are our truest selves in "those moments when self-consciousness fades away and a person is lost in a challenge, a cause, the love of another or the love of God."[3]

When as Christians we speak of love, we are speaking of *ultimate* love. We ultimately love the thing we orient our existence around. Or one could say we pledge our allegiance to that which we ultimately love.

Think back on the patriotic words so often rehearsed in early education. We don't ever really pledge allegiance to a mere flag, do we? We pledge allegiance to what the flag represents—a vision of the good life. A vision, for instance, that may create room for justice and prosperity. People often believe this vision is encapsulated in a national ideology. Christians believe it's contained in the kingdom of God.

Our vision of the good life is always just that . . . a vision. In the spirit of Descartes we may try to make the kingdom of God about propositions, but what we are really proposing is a vision—a picture. We don't ultimately love or pledge our allegiance to an *idea* of the good life. Plainly put, we love what we picture.

Pictures are powerful and a direct product of our imaginations. I can think of several movies in which the protagonist resolves the central conflict by stumbling onto some profound truth contained within, of all things, a book. Stay with me on this. The hero lifts a heavy, ancient volume onto a creaky desk in a forgotten back room. After blowing away layers of dust, he opens the book to what? A picture. Always a picture. Though the books in these movies are enormous in size and contain thousands of words, it's always a picture that resolves the conflict and makes

As it turns out,
we aren't the first
ones to make a case for
art and faith.

the audience go "ah-ha!" It's almost funny when you think about it. What are all the pages for?

Scripture, of course, goes to great lengths to paint pictures of the good life: streets of gold, walls of jasper, a beautiful bride, among others. These kinds of portrayals move us because we are fundamentally affective creatures, not ultimately motivated by mere ideas. Whether or not we're conscious of it, our ultimate loves are formed around pictures that have the aesthetic power to make us feel something.

The value of art and artists is implicit in this conversation. Pictures of the good life are communicated most powerfully in stories, legends, myths, plays, novels, and film rather than dissertations, messages, and monographs.[4] There is certainly a time and place for cognitive material (like this book), but nothing pierces our hearts and permeates our bones like paintings, stories, and music.

One of the reasons Christianity is so compelling is because our faith doesn't rest on arbitrary thoughts or random verses. God has communicated to us through a grand narrative. His story paints a beautiful mosaic of characters and pictures that shape our ultimate love.

As it turns out, we aren't the first ones to make a case for art and faith.

- What does being human mean to you?

- How would the overall conception of humanity be different if Descartes had said, "I *love,* therefore I am"? How might the world look differently today if this were the case?

- Which do you think motivates you more: what you think or what you love? Give an example from your life revealing how this is true.

- Describe your picture of "the good life."

- What artistic works contribute to your sense of hope?

THE ORGAN OF MEANING

"Unless we are creators,
we are not fully alive."
—*Madeleine L'Engle*

What was Israel's chief sin throughout their ancient history?

Forgetting the Lord their God.

So what are we to think when we read in 1 Samuel that God's choice for a king over this forgetful people was not a strong warrior but an artist—a poet-musician?

Perhaps Israel was suffering from a crisis of imagination. If the current Evangelical culture is any indication, today's church seems to be suffering from the same.

I believe a healthy and vital imagination may very well be the single most important component in our endeavor to be humans who fully embody and re-*member* our belief. C. S. Lewis calls our imagination "the organ of meaning,"[1] suggesting that words only take on meaning when we apply *images* to them. Imagination then, Lewis understood, is formational, preceding language and subsequently our understanding of truth.[2]

We can amass facts and information. We can memorize dogma. Regardless of how sound our doctrine, unless it means something to us—that is, unless it is intuitively pictured or experienced—then to a great degree it is behaviorally inconsequential. Without good imaginations our faith is largely impotent to bring about transformation in our lives.

Imagination changes behavior. Why do animated polar bears slide on ice while enjoying Coca-Cola? Why do geckos sell insurance? or talking babies help investors? There's a reason so much money is invested in shaping the public imagination. Artists and marketers alike know that imagination is the engine that drives decisions and lifestyles. Capture and provoke someone's imagination, and you've changed the person's brand loyalty.

Far more essential paradigms can be altered than those of buying habits. For instance, I have a friend who used to read a lot of information about poverty in third world countries. Although he knew the statistics and had what you would consider an inherent curiosity, it wasn't until after he saw *Slumdog Millionaire* that he was on a plane to Africa to immerse himself in the plight of starving people. What happened to change him? A work of artistic expression pierced his imagination and gave meaning to the information in his head. There are, of course, endless such stories.

Our imaginations are living organisms. They are continually in the process of being formed whether we realize it or not. Everything contributes. Everything matters. The question is never *if* our imaginations are formed, the question is always *how*. A child will grow regardless of whether he or she has attentive parents. Left unattended, one can assume a child will be informed by alternative and somewhat arbitrary narratives. On the other end of the spectrum, if a parent manipulates and assert too much control, the results are equally dangerous. In either case, the child's growth will most likely be stunted and deformed.

As the church, are we properly nurturing our corporate imagination? What consideration does "the organ of meaning" typically receive in our congregations today?

"Oh no.
We've done
the imagining for you."

BOXY IMAGINATIONS

In a recent episode of *The Simpsons,* Lisa wants to buy some Legos. She wants the Lego set I remember from my childhood: a box full of random Lego pieces with no instructions or blueprints. But to her dismay, the only Lego sets Lisa finds at the toy store are those parents and children today are familiar with: preconceived Lego designs built to look like the picture on the box.

Lisa protests, "But what if I want to build my own thing?" The store clerk glibly responds, "Oh no. We've done the imagining for you."

A friend of mine once saw the music sheets used by a large metropolitan church. He was shocked to find there were actually notes in the margins that told the singers exactly when to close their eyes and raise their hands. Included were directions for when to "really sing from the heart."

The best imagining comes from the shared effort and participation of a community. Yet instead of doing the hard work to cultivate and mature the imaginations of our members, we often do the imagining for them. Where is the participation? Are there no more kids running around creating original masterpieces with Legos?

Sunday gatherings are an imagination-shaping event and one of the most significant functions of weekly worship. Regardless of what a worship service looks like, I assure you it profoundly shapes imagination. Again the question is not if we are being formed, but how. Our answer to this question is hugely consequential not only to individuals and congregations, but to our neighbors as well. We must think in terms this expansive considering the church's mandate and responsibility to bring about the kingdom on earth.

Art is largely about forming the personal and collective imagination; for this reason, artists believe their craft carries significant consequence. (This must be why so many of them are willing to live into the very real stereotype of "starving artist.") Instead, what passes as art in our worship services often comes with a heavy-handed agenda, leaving little room for imagination, questions, and mystery. We make it difficult for our parishioners to even *feel* in a way that's not dictated from up front. "You should feel this way . . ." we say in so many words.

The problem is that when people are prevented from having honest conversations with God about their doubts and griefs, they begin to feel misunderstood by him—a relational chasm forms between creature and Creator. As pastors, it is not enough to read provocative Scripture passages—like those in the Psalms—if we do not equip our members with a similar ability to express their longings. We do a disservice by teaching them that God is big enough for certain emotions in the human experience, but not all of them.

Furthermore, what our worship services lack in emotional creativity, we don't necessarily make up for in physical creativity. Consider some Western church trends in recent years. We often congregate in gymnasiums, sit in perfect rows, and passively listen to someone talk at us for thirty minutes. The sermon is cerebral in nature and appeals to our logical selves. Musically we insist on limiting ourselves to two rather stale categories: traditional and contemporary. In many gatherings the only thing we're offered to hold and touch are bulletins.

I want to stress that none of this is inherently wrong, but it does lack something of the creative participation that ultimately shapes our imagination. We are made in the image—imagination—of God, but we must ask ourselves what kind of meaning we are giving this picture. When we fail as a church to be good image-bearers and culture-shapers, people will go looking for more compelling pictures elsewhere. A worship service is an opportunity for liturgical engagement, responsiveness, and reflection. It is a place where we make room to interact with wonder. What of our invitation to create with him? When do we participate and not merely receive (beyond singing, that is)? Do we engage all our senses; that is, our smell, touch, and taste? At what point do we slow down and take stock of our feelings?

Although in some cases Christians may become biblically proficient and morally respectable, if C. S. Lewis is right and imagination is the organ of meaning, then many of us are currently in a very dangerous and somewhat precarious position. Rehearsing and habituating our faith in an imaginative way is how we embody its meaning; it's the first step toward comprehending our love.

When we do not know what we love, we flounder in our everyday decision making. Floundering is not a proper vision for humanity. God makes and intends for us to flourish.

MISFITS AND USE-LESS

Examining the larger context in which the church finds itself is irreducibly important to our ecclesial critique. In an effort to outproduce, outpace, and out-manufacture the competition, our Western culture has become increasingly bottom-line. Institutions of higher learning promote what are commonly called the hard sciences, those areas of study that rely on quantifiable data, scientific method, and complete objectivity. The importance placed on these disciplines is reflected in the way graduates of the hard sciences are rewarded vocationally and monetarily in public life.

Vocations and fields of study that allow for variables and subjectivity, including the arts, are routinely relegated to the margins of culture. Outside of a few extraordinary exceptions involving celebrity, they are not promoted or recognized as approaching the hard sciences in value or consequence.

The arts and the sciences are not inherently disparate; our culture, however, increasingly lives into a reality that reduces our understanding of "real" or "useful" to mean only that which can be used for profit. Those vocations not appearing to have any practical function or explicit financial worth are continually ignored or swept aside.

As is too often the case, the church has followed the dominant culture's lead and promoted a faith that is more focused on increasing functionality than fostering a faithful imagination—a picture of the good life in God. Consequentially, we are often able to operate an impressive number of programs, but look strikingly similar to the rest of the world in values, priorities, and actual behavior. Our spiritual filters are utilitarian and even slightly mathematical. In the name of evangelism we speak of people as "projects" and adopt banking language to describe the merit of "investing" in someone. Having our imaginations shaped in purely functional directions, we even begin to judge each other's spiritual health according to its productivity. All of a sudden we talk about ourselves as "bad Christians" (assuming there is such a beast) or "good Christians" (perhaps an even more dangerous beast).

I'm increasingly convinced that people don't decide to join churches in order to submit their imaginations around something extraordinary; neither do I think their intention is to learn the practice of communal contemplation or reflection. What I find is that, increasingly, people decide to attend churches for very pragmatic and quantifiable reasons: a singles group, a scene to meet people and make friends, a youth group to keep kids off drugs, and so forth. The list is endless.

The various reasons for choosing churches are understandable and, in many cases, perfectly acceptable. Only when pastors and church leaders cater to this pragmatism do we encounter a problem. The bad habit of measuring success using quantifiable data is absorbed directly from surrounding cultural trends. It is the lynchpin that ultimately has determined art's fate in the local church. Art and imagination aren't easily quantifiable, yet we cannot underestimate their influence and ability to environ us.

Founder and creative director of the International Arts Movement, Makoto Fujimura, coined the term "use-less" art when addressing the need for artists to resist rampant cultural utilitarianism. In a call for artists (including those in the church) to be "misfits in a utilitarian society,"[3] he commends us to draw attention to the many facets of reality that don't provide immediate services.

Fujimura speaks to the importance of experiencing art as an end in and of itself. The end, he implies, is every place in which we meet God. "We cannot 'use' the arts, any more than we can 'use' a human being. This pervasive utilitarian view is a symptom of our greater cultural malaise, a view that can dehumanize the entire river of culture."

He continues, "The heartbeat of the arts resounds with internal significance that quietly pleads for art to be more than a mere tool."[4] The same could be said of our faith; our relationship with God is more than a mere tool.

Interactions with that which is artistic, beautiful, and good can help us find worth and value in a "use-less" faith. When we

When we begin
to sense and are
awakened to the gratuitous
nature of the world given, we can
potentially imagine ourselves apart
from what we contribute
or produce.

begin to sense and are awakened to the gratuitous nature of the world given, we can potentially imagine ourselves apart from what we contribute or produce. Art can restore meaning to our faith by providing us visions of God that transcend language itself. Artists ignite our collective imagination to the extraordinarily beautiful and lovely.

Back to the part of the story where David is appointed as king over the Israelites. We are made to wonder if there was a greater task for Israel than fighting wars or achieving some sort of quantifiable position as a world power. Perhaps the king's chief task was one of forming the collective imagination in order to help the people remember what it is to be human, made in the image of God.

- What kind of artistic mediums move you? When is a time you remember being emotionally moved by a work of creativity?

- Describe the role imagination plays in your own faith journey.

- Do you think today's church often does the imagining for us? If so, how have you experienced this?

- Describe what you think the term *"use-less"* art means.

- How could a *"use-less"* faith be formative? How would it possibly make us *misfits*?

MYSTERY-DEPRIVED WORLD

"Science is no more than an investigation
of a miracle we can never explain, and art is an
interpretation of that miracle."

—*Ray Bradbury*

Consider this quote from famed science fiction author, H. G. Wells:

> There was a time when my little soul shone and was uplifted by the starry enigma of the sky. That has now disappeared. I go out and look at the stars in the same way I look at wallpaper.

What, exactly, has happened to H. G. Wells' amazed "little soul"? Does this quote have anything to say about who we are as a people? Are we as a culture increasingly dulled in our condition? Are we seeing wallpaper?

At the very least, Wells' quote reminds me of the profound loss of mystery I feel on a daily basis. I intuitively crave mystery. I love standing before something I know is bigger than me, something that I just can't fathom or grasp. I don't think I'm alone.

Last summer my family took a detour driving home from the Rocky Mountains to see the famed Royal Gorge—a natural canyon encompassing the Arkansas River that is reportedly 50 feet wide and 1,250 feet deep. I remember seeing it as a kid, and I couldn't wait to let my children stand at the edge (not too close) of something profound. When we arrived I couldn't believe the changes that had taken place since my childhood visit. The place was completely commercialized. People were paying fifty dollars a pop just to get through a gate and stare at the wonder of it all.

Some kindly stranger in the parking lot pulled me aside and said, "Hey, if you walk up the hill a bit, there's a hole in the fence where you can peek through." There we were, noses glued to a fence hole in order to save a couple bucks, trying to glimpse something mysterious and grand. And while we didn't have the whole picture, we saw enough to send us staggering. It got me thinking later that the whole operation must take in ten grand a day from people just trying to stand at the edge of something that—at least to us—seemed beyond explanation.

I'm not alone. At some basic level we crave mystery. And, as exampled above, we also crave to lean into mystery. By standing as close to the edge as possible and pulling our noses up to the fence, we found ourselves joining with people who have for all of time said, "Let us get a glimpse of the thing!" In this way I'm reminded that mystery does not prompt unknowing but rather draws us nearer to itself and begs a closer look.

In Scripture we also get an idea of what it's like to lean into God's mystery. There is at once a sense of awe and intimacy portrayed in biblical literature when people simply looked at the sky, the mountains, or the ocean. They seemed to be with Wells on this one: the sky was a "starry enigma" and brought them to their knees. In the Bible, we don't hear about people using study books and discipleship courses in order to learn humility. Awe and humility seem to be self-evident—a state of being. What has changed?

There was a time when standing in the presence of the Holy and Sacred meant standing in the presence of great mystery. Worship and fear of God were intuitively experienced, not heady subjects teased out in thirty-minute lectures. God was truly awful —full of awe—and faith was marked by the kind of mystery that surpasses language.

What we find now is a pervading belief that a person can achieve the whole mystery. The result of which is obtaining a god in our heads who isn't all that impressive, for the very reason that he is obtainable. Our skulls have become thicker and our knees no longer bend. We've lost our posture of humility, not to mention that we've got him wrong.

What is faith and who have we made God out to be in our increasingly pragmatic, functional, and scientifically-driven culture?

I remember sitting through one particular college ministry small group in which the leader passed out a questionnaire reading, "How certain are you that you will go to heaven when you die?" Of course I knew the *right* answer. But after an hour of sitting in a circle with fellow sophomore boys quietly absorbing everything our leader had to say and obediently filling in my workbook with pat answers, the whole thing was growing monotonous. I was weary of towing the line.

I had a lot of confidence that heaven was somewhere in my future, but the question specifically asked about my certainty.

In answering, I wasn't so much fighting the idea that God cared about my eternity as I was trying (on a largely subconscious level at the time) to honor the mystery that says, "I'm not God, so let's leave certainty out of this." I didn't want to believe that someone could cement something as mysteriously beautiful as heaven into a mere proposition.

Like I said, I knew the right answer, but something about the calculated Bible study reawakened within me a deeply buried desire for the sort of faith that prompts a man to fall on his face and plead ignorance. I was interested in a kind of seeing and hearing that required kneeling.

I wrote down 97 percent.

The leader's eyes lit up like Christmas lights. I was immediately confronted with a series of Bible verses *guaranteeing* my eternal salvation. With nothing further, the leader sat back and said, "So you see, Jon, you can be 100 percent certain of your eternity with Jesus." That was it. No more conversation. All matters of uncertainty settled. The circle of sophomore guys simultaneously lowered their eyes to the workbook on their laps and moved on to the next question.

We have become so obsessed with certainty that we've lost the more important matter at hand—love. Relational love. Anne Lamott says it this way:

> I have a lot of faith. But I am also afraid a lot, and have no real certainty about anything. I remember something Father

Tom had told me—that the opposite of faith is not doubt, but certainty. Certainty is missing the point entirely. Faith includes the mess, the emptiness and discomfort, and lets it be there until some light returns.[1]

In place of a humble and honest relationship with God we settle for a pale love affair with formulas and easy propositions concerning the matters of our faith. We've turned the Bible into a Complete Idiot's Guide to eternal salvation.

By believing we have achieved God and God-thought, we have actually stopped seeking him. If we say good-bye to mystery in favor of "truth," we actually dim our understanding of his greatness.

Let me be the first to give certainty and scientific objectivity its proper due. Both art and faith have benefited from scientific knowledge and careful observation of the consistent rhythms of the universe. Likewise, science and technology have benefited from faith. Though too simply stated, the realms of art, faith, and science are best understood when comprehended by one another. The problem occurs when the church fragments reality by ripping apart science and art—the rational and intuitive—favoring one over the other. In a modern fast-paced culture that pursues efficiency and simplicity at all cost, the appeals to rational win out. When art and science are not held in tension with one another, mystery is often forgotten and left behind.

It is not ignorance that yields awe, but the *knowing* of something greater than ourselves.

In reality, the world still holds a vast amount of mystery, not in spite of technology and scientific advances, but because of them. It is not ignorance that yields awe, but the *knowing* of something greater than ourselves. There are wonders on the micro and macro levels alike, and for the first time in history we have the tools to observe them up close. Astronomers are now able to look in distances of light-years. New planets are still being discovered (and old ones dismissed). We are finding evidence of black holes in the solar system. A person can actually observe a star as it burns out. At the end of all our investigation, we find not less mystery and awe, but more. Every answer to a question prompts a hundred other questions. We receive the scientific witness and ask what it means for us when even in the natural world there is entropy, grief, and death . . . but also endlessly more life than we first perceived.

Divine revelation is seeing the mystery. The mystery is everywhere.

We often think of revelation as a one-time event: history. Understood as something in the past that should be studied and analyzed, we are content to merely remember when revelation used to happen. But what if revelation is ongoing? What if divine revelation isn't so much something we historically understand but something in which we participate? Scientist and philosopher Michael Polanyi says that the success of scientific genius is an ability to dwell inside of a thing "that is more art than science, more poetry than prose, more spirit than rational control of the data. And more letting go than holding on."[2]

Rather than avoid or explain away the mysteries of life and the universe, what if faith is supposed to help us embrace them?

TENSION ANYONE?

Mystery isn't easy. It doesn't have much to do with the golden grails of our culture: efficiency, comfort, and simplicity. In fact, it's extremely uncomfortable because it is without reassurances or simple solutions. Mystery invites tension, and we are culturally conditioned to avoid tension at all cost. The popular flight from tension, and the accompanying pursuit of comfort, is reflected in our current debt crisis and modern dietary habits. It is also reflected by the way we have become consumers of faith.

Although we are accustomed to avoiding tension, it is not inherently evil. In fact, most aerodynamics engineers will tell us that tension is exactly what is necessary to keep an airplane flying. Furthermore, I don't have to be an engineer to know the reason the hammock in my backyard works is because of the tension supporting it between two trees. Tension, as preached by the pastors of science, isn't always bad. Sometimes it's necessary. Once again we learn something about our humanity from the laws of the natural world around us. We know that tension is necessary for flying; perhaps it is also necessary for true human flourishing. Here's what I mean:

Art doesn't always deal in the realm of what is obvious; its preferred dealings are with those things that are implied or might be.

A prevailing theological assumption is that we are made in the Creator's image and, therefore, have the capacity to be creators ourselves. No doubt. The problem is that few of us create just by telling ourselves to—we require some sort of impetus. Tension, being in its very nature uncomfortable and unresolved, provokes us toward engagement and prompts creativity. Tension provides us the necessary stimuli to live into the image of a God who continually creates and sustains wonderfully majestic and redemptive works.

The essence of redemption is restoring to health that which is unhealthy and making broken things whole. How can we live faithfully into the image of a redemptive God if we're constantly ignoring tension and glossing over brokenness? Certainty preserves a false sense of efficiency and comfort, but it kills our creativity.

Look around at a bookstore, a theater, or a gallery. Good art flows from brokenness. Beautiful colors come from smashed pigments. The best stories come from broken dreams. Art is closely allied with redemption in that it requires honesty about pain, brokenness, and death. You can't have one without the other. This is glorious tension at its best.

As the church—a people seeking to embody truth—it's worthwhile to pause and consider what kind of art we promote versus what kind of art we find offensive. Are we allowing for tension?

If I'm ever offended by art, it usually has nothing to do with darkness, evil, or malevolence, so long as it isn't gratuitous. What I find most offensive is when brokenness gets glossed over and reality is portrayed through a falsely sanitized lens. (Scripture certainly never pulls this trick!) Good art is thoughtful in that it at least hints at the whole story. Honesty about pain allows artists to, in a sense, prepare the way for hope and newness.

Art doesn't always deal in the realm of what is obvious; its preferred dealings are with those things that are implied or might be. In the same way our bodies (seen) imply spirit (unseen), art points beyond to a deeper reality and stimulates imagination. Questions and doubts are a part of life. If we allow it to, however, art can help us become joyful and skilled in our articulation of tension, a by-product of which is good fellowship and conversation. If our faiths don't ultimately rest on propositions, we won't be threatened by challenging dialogue and diverse ideas.

Seeking to get out from under a rational imperative, Jesus primarily taught through storytelling. His narratives weren't easy to understand or comfortable to live within, thus making it difficult for a listener to rationalize his or her way into safety. By using the art form of narrative, Christ was able to pierce the people's imaginations and reveal their subconscious loves. How ironic that pastors today often imagine their role as the exact opposite–to eliminate tension and provide comfort.

Of course, comfort isn't all bad. We are hardwired to seek it. There is a time and place for lounging in our favorite chair with a cold beverage. However, I have found—and I think it's somewhat universally true—that the best and most rewarding periods of relaxation come after, or at least alongside of, seasons of hard work.

I love the way "rest" and "work" are performed in conjunction with each other in what is commonly called the parable of the talents (Matthew 25). Amid various interpretations of this parable, one thing always stands out: good rest is linked with good work.

Contrary to popular notions, art itself is not romantic as much as it is hard work. We are often fooled into thinking that art is purely inspiration. A common misconception is that artists don't work, they play; people believe that upon sitting down an artist can automatically create something beautiful.

I remember the first time I wrote for a publisher. Up until that time I thought of myself as a writer. I turned in the first draft and was basically told to rewrite the whole thing. The second draft didn't fare much better. By the fourth and fifth drafts I was practically paralyzed from the great tragedy of it all, convinced that I would never be a writer. Truthfully, it takes work and a certain amount of tension to create anything worthwhile and lasting. It also takes time.

RUSH HOUR

Mystery, like beauty, is something that requires pause. When something loses its mystery, we ignore it. And the opposite is true as well. When we do not take the time to ponder something, it can remain as beautiful as ever, but it will disappear from our notice and sight. We stop seeing the stars. We're not aware of the flower garden. We ignore our spouse. In order for mystery to remain mysterious, it requires a certain submission and commitment to stay and just be. Both mystery and beauty harbor a depth of luminosity that requires and rewards patient contemplation.

One of the most complimentary things I tell my wife is that she's a mystery to me. Now this could be taken as an affront, or as me telling her that I don't understand her complexity and so I give up. But my wife knows that what I mean is the opposite. By calling her a mystery, I'm declaring that there are riches in her I haven't even glimpsed. I'm pronouncing my desire to stay put and just be in her presence. When I quit trying to figure her out and simply listen, I am essentially saying, *You are something to experience, not to be owned or dominated.*

If it feels difficult to simply exist and experience, it may be because we are so conditioned to rush and accomplish. While it's wholly proper to accomplish tasks, and sometimes it's even necessary to rush, these make for bad cultural virtues. Accomplishment, success, and achievement are so magnified today that the very ability to pause, reflect, and listen has nearly disappeared.

Consider the story of Joshua Bell and L'Enfant Plaza.

Joshua Bell is a master violinist who regularly plays sold-out concerts with many of the world's leading orchestras and conductors. In 2007 the *Washington Post* decided to conduct an experiment in which they asked Bell to don a baseball cap and stand in front of the subway station playing his violin. For nearly an hour the world's most famous violinist became a street urchin of sorts.

There he stood baring his magnificent soul in what was essentially a free concert for all the people rushing to work on that January morning. Of course, it was only a concert for anyone who would stop and listen. In order to appreciate what was happening, a person had to slow down and submit. Therein lies the meaning of the experiment. Virtually no one stopped. Reportedly, only a handful of people paused to notice him out of approximately 1,100 passing pedestrians.

One person who did recognize him, a demographer with the Commerce Department, said of the event, "It was the most astonishing thing I've ever seen in Washington. Joshua Bell was standing there playing at rush hour, and people were not stopping, and not even looking, and some were flipping quarters at him. Quarters! I wouldn't do that to anybody. I was thinking, Omigosh, what kind of a city do I live in that this could happen?"[3]

Makoto Fujimura offers an answer: "What kind of city do we live in? Well, it's clear from the experiment that it is not the kind that recognizes beauty so readily."

Rush hour doesn't facilitate the receptive and submissive posture necessary for recognizing beauty. Neither does it encourage the appreciation of "a universe full of hidden mysteries and micro realities that seem extravagant and excessive."[4]

Art, having meaning that transcends language, requires us to slow down and experience. The same can be said for our relationship with God.

- How do you feel about the idea of a "mysterious" God and a faith that embraces the unknown?

- Why do you think it's so easy to lose a sense of mystery?

- Is there a connection between mystery and beauty? How have you seen this in your own life?

- How do you distinguish between certainty and confidence?

- Describe how brokenness is necessary for redemption. Why is brokenness an essential ingredient in art?

• How do you usually react to tension? Is there a healthy place for tension in your faith journey?

• What are some things that you could do to intentionally slow down in life? What might you have to give up?

4

METHOD MATTERS

"We become what we behold.
We shape our tools and then
our tools shape us."
—*Marshall McLuhan*

A friend of mine recently experimented with small group curriculum for his church. He decided to have people work their way through a new and popular series on spiritual formation. The books were designed for small groups, easy to read, and, conveniently, completely stocked with suggestions about structuring a profitable discussion around each chapter.

Everything seemed to be going smoothly with my friend's curriculum decision. People were somewhat engaged and nearly half of his church ordered the book. This might not sound impressive, but getting half of the church somewhat engaged in anything is a smashing success. I was interested in introducing the book to my own fledgling church.

And then my friend quit using the book series.

I was confused. The whole thing seemed to be working. Why quit?

When I asked my friend about his reason for abandoning the project, I wasn't completely prepared for his response. He shrugged his shoulders and simply said, "The book wasn't very well written."

"What?"

"It wasn't, you know, very good literature."

I didn't have to ask any more questions.

This particular friend and I were in the middle of our own personal small group. We were reading Jack Kerouac's American classic *On the Road* and finding common ground in the book's prose and rich characters. It was serving as a kind of cautionary tale for a couple of pastors who were slightly prone to sadness and madness ourselves.

In fact, it's usually an internal struggle for me to leave such imaginative writing in order to read the comparatively dry pages of so much well-intentioned Christian literature. I miss the craft. I miss the artistry. It's often easier for me to grow, reflect, and even pray when engaged in works of popular literature. In some ways I feel like I live a dual life in this respect, but of course this isn't true. (That's one reason why Beggars Table is formed around the word *seamless.* God is everywhere!)

When my friend explained why he quit the whole curriculum campaign, I actually felt a sense of relief. It confirmed a certain angst I had about adapting the stuff to my church and in a weird way I felt justified. It wasn't good literature. Awesome.

"You know, Jon," he continued, "method matters." He leaned in to whisper his deep mystery, "The medium is the message."

My friend believed he was doing his church a disservice and failing to represent God appropriately by leading them through something that, although well-informed, wasn't imaginatively and skillfully created. The significance of his artistic leadership is poignant.

Perhaps the means, mediums, and methods we employ actually communicate as much about God as the actual content itself. By this I mean that it is possible we intuitively receive more of the gospel through methods than we are aware.

I used to work for a church that continually distinguished between "function" and "form." "Function" was the word used to refer to message or content, and "form" represented whichever medium we chose to communicate this content. The idea, then, was that we could legitimately change forms, but function was to stay the same.

I wrestle with this "forms are malleable but function is fixed" principal. By asserting that the same message can be taught through any method, it felt as though our leaders were saying, "Choose any form you want as long as you adapt it to your target audience. It won't affect the inherent message. We all ultimately hear the same thing . . . just in different clothes."

After years of pastoring and observing the responses of people in my church, I'm not sure this is true. Besides being absurdly compelling, good form has its own distinguishing message. Our methods are more than just creative conduits for the important stuff, they are part and parcel of the story itself. I am more and more convinced that the package shapes (or fails to shape) our imaginations around an image of God as much as anything we say or don't say.

SPACE SPEAKS

"It doesn't matter where we meet. We can worship anywhere."

I'm familiar with this sentiment and, without a doubt, it contains some truth. But there is another side to this particular coin.

Where we meet does matter. Space matters. We must believe that it matters to God too, or else the excessive beauty and granular detail of the world around us wouldn't exist.

A highly respected teacher used to fly in from the coast once every month in order to stand before a bunch of us and unpack some of those insights and philosophies that are able to expand the imagination. We explored such ideas as breaking down the secular/sacred barrier, living a public faith, and calling the church out of Christian ghettos. It was always a wonderful discussion and something to anticipate every month.

But the meetings had an awkward element. A local church hosted the event and insisted on us meeting in the youth room (a space in the church often designated safe for new ideas). As typical of a church youth room, there were posters everywhere, almost all of them depicting the latest Christian pop band. Strewn about the room were fashionable items directly from the Christian subculture that prompted me during our meetings to wonder what Jesus *would* do. Having a conversation about emerging from the Christian ghetto in that room? It was disconcerting.

Here is a prime example of our artistic poverty, I thought as I sat there. *We even underestimate the discernment of our youth!* Rather than providing a good, artful narrative, we seem to be offering instead a poor man's version of what popular culture is already providing, plus sanitation. If this youth space was any reflection, we are giving these kids—the future church—a less than compelling liturgy.

Managers of restaurants understand the importance of atmosphere, decoration, and spatial ethos. So do owners of coffee shops and theaters. Homeowners also realize that space makes a statement, and they invest time and thought into what they want their home to "say" about their family. The church needs to live into the same reality. The actual space in which a church gathers forms the collective imagination. Every physical space tells a story about a community's posture toward stewardship, artisanship, and worship. What's your church's story? What kind of message are you sending?

A COUNTERCULTURAL MESSAGE

I remember a conversation in which a friend of mine was expressing concern about the lack of quality art in today's church.

"Jon, five hundred years ago, the church was the epicenter for art and artists. Painters and philosophers came to the church for inspiration. Churches gathered in beautiful cathedrals. What's happened? Why is art so marginalized in the church? Why is the artistic bar for the church so low now? People say, 'Well, it's fine for a *church*.'"

My friend was excited to get a conversation going about how we can begin to value art in the church once again. In particular, he wanted to talk about what it would mean to recapture the inspiration of old cathedrals. And while I was enthused about our exchange, I had one piece of advice.

"You're going to have to scratch a bit deeper," I said.

"What do you mean?"

"If you want to uncover what's wrong with the church, then you have to begin with examining the wider culture. Uncover how the culture feels about art and you have a clue as to what is happening within the church."

Like it or not, the church has a habit of mirroring the wider culture. And vice versa. It's a symbiotic relationship in which the church adopts cultural values and the culture often amplifies the malfunctions of the church. Too often the church adopts cultural ideals of success, health, and prosperity and simply co-opts them to "fit" Jesus.

Even the ancient cathedrals my friend so greatly admired weren't free from the embellished cultural values of their day. Within their very architecture and artwork, these cathedrals depicted sanctification and heaven in ways that "reproduced rather than subverted the separation of laity from clergy and the peasantry from the aristocracy and the monarchy."[1] Consider the painting above the great door of Chartres. In this beautiful depiction of heavenly ascent, the saints and upper class patrons appear almost thinned out as they float upward to heaven while peasants and artisans are depicted sweating in solid form below.

Space matters. We must believe that it matters to God too, or else the excessive beauty and granular detail of the world around us wouldn't exist.

Commenting on post WWII German cathedrals, Philip Sheldrake says the various attempts to capture a new holistic vision of humanity after the appalling experiences of National Socialism and the disintegration of Germany actually function in retrospect as, "genuinely historic insights or an expression of a late-twentieth-century spiritual angst."[2]

Our churches, even our buildings, mirror what's going on in the surrounding culture. To understand why art isn't valued in the church requires an analysis of the value of art in the broader culture. Such an analysis is only a matter of looking around in order to identify one of modernity's most visible cultural phenomenon—suburban sprawl. It's a trend that affects most Americans in one way or another, and nowhere is it more prevalent than in my hometown, Kansas City.

Kansas City is known for fantastic barbeque and jazz music. It's also known for rapid and seemingly limitless suburban sprawl. In the last decade our ten fastest growing residential areas have all been fringe areas. Likewise, the neighborhoods that have experienced the most residential loss have all been urban areas. Kansas City is among the nation's leaders for sheer rate of sprawl, and this is more than a recent trend. In some ways, Kansas City embraces sprawl in its very planning and identity. Sprawl is part of our cultural ethos.

Kansas City's airport was built miles away from its downtown anticipating unrestrained sprawl. Our city boasts the nation's first shopping district built specifically for suburban pedestrians. Our sports complexes are located outside of the urban core and, like suburban strip malls, share an extensive parking lot.

Though we are looking critically at suburban migration, it's important to remember suburbs aren't the problem. In fact, the very idea of the suburb comes from a redemptive push against the dehumanization that occurred during the Industrial Era; originally suburbs were the infrastructural effort to restore man's dignity. There is, however, a difference between the suburbs in general and the phenomenon we call suburban sprawl. Sprawl indicates an unchecked and almost reckless expansion. Most of these expansions are not well planned or concerned for the urban core of a city, and thus older neighborhoods are left with decay and crime. Another attribute of sprawl is the disregard for beauty. In the name of efficient and cheap housing, and in an attempt to capitalize on such culturally-bred virtues as comfort, ease, and safety, we have constructed in our suburban neighbor-hoods poorly made homes that tend to look exactly the same. Even our strip malls could easily be swapped out for other strip malls without anyone noticing.

These observations are important because there is arguably no better way to determine what a culture values than to con-sider where its people live, how they live, and why they live that way. Given these guidelines, there is little question where our cul-ture stands on efficiency, convenience, and comfort. Yet these are not values that assign worth to creation or to human beings. These qualities do not nearly assist in the formation of awe.

In reference to my friend's concern about today's church, there is a fair amount of risk if we mean to honestly hold beauty and art up against our conventional understanding of church growth, evangelism, and cultural models of success. If the methods matter and if restoring and creating beauty is the church's artistic calling, then it's important to note that we are being tasked with something that is—at least in part—countercultural. It's not that our society is ugly or anti-beauty in every aspect, but as I have indicated before, fostering beauty flies in the face of deep-seated cultural assumptions.

THE COMMUNITY ARTIST

Beggars Table sacrifices a lot of convenience and practicality in order to meet in our gallery. We can't be too uptight about proximity to other people, for instance. Congregating in a space full of beauty, one in which imaginative work is continually being exchanged for new imaginative work, speaks volumes about God's ongoing redemption and revelation. Whether or not people are aware of it, this curatorial metaphor has a potentially profound effect on their formation.

The church needs artists to come out from the margins and actively lead in the spiritual formation of its people. Filmmakers know *how* a frame is shot matters and painters know that the

The church needs artists to come out from the margins and actively lead in the spiritual formation of its people.

process through which paint is applied is, to a large degree, what they want to say.

Artists know a universal truth that is often missing in today's utilitarian driven church. Methods matter. Consider the many Old Testament passages we habitually ignore in which God gives instruction on framing and building his temple. God seems to stress that the dimensions, materials, and architecture of his temple are significant in and of themselves. They say something important about him.

There is an implied challenge in this conversation for pastors and church leaders. While I'm extremely sympathetic to the constant demand placed on pastors to excel in different disciplines—no doubt pastors are required to wear many hats—how often do pastors imagine one of their hats to be "community artist"? Would such a title free us up to exercise more creative liberty? I think nothing has more potential to ignite the church's imagination than for pastors to become attuned to the importance of method and medium.

In *Surprised by Hope*, author N. T. Wright encourages the church to imagine itself as the world's manifest artist, and to become the place "in every town and village where new creativity bursts forth for the whole community, pointing to the hope that, like all beauty, always comes as a surprise."[3]

- Give some thought to the various methods used to facilitate communication and ideas (in the media, schools, businesses, etc.). Why do you think these particular methods are used?

- Now give some thought to the methods you've experienced in different ministries and churches. Spend some time discussing what those specific methods communicate about God, faith, and truth.

- Does the bifurcation of "form" and "function" make sense to you? Why do you think this divide is tempting for church leaders?

- If you attend a weekly church gathering, what story does your space tell?

- Describe a work of art where the method itself spoke meaningfully to you.

5
SHAPING THE LENS

"A mirror may not reflect mind, but a man's response to landscapes, faces, events does. My skewed vision was that of a man looking at himself by looking at what he looks at."

—*William Least Heat-Moon*

We all have a lens through which we see the world. Helping us make sense of things, this lens allows us to process different events, information, and people who come across our paths. The way we see the world as determined by our personal lens is often referred to as our "worldview."

Most of us remain largely ignorant of our worldview lens, unaware that we see reality through a lens at all. We simply assume that what we see and how we process information is universal and accurate. Unfortunately, this is often and especially true in the religious sector because of our emphasis on certainty. And, largely unbeknownst to us, our worldviews are usually shaped by the surrounding culture and adapted to our faith rather than the other way around.

A worldview gives us a tremendous sense of security and is immediately reflected in our behavior and morality. Because worldview goes deeper than mere ideology, most of us don't want to question and examine our respective glasses and become angry toward anyone who suggests we do so. It's no coincidence that so many people were livid at Jesus throughout his lifetime.

Our worldview lens affects everything, from the most quotidian of tasks to some of our grand-scale decisions. We bring them with us to schools, art galleries, movies, and conversations. We read Scripture through our lenses, and they greatly determine what we hear and don't hear the Bible say.

You can't escape your worldview, but you can become aware of its presence. And then, upon measuring it up against the gospel and kingdom, you can change it.

Changing worldviews is a monumental task that requires great sensitivity and patience. It doesn't happen overnight. If not provoked by a sudden and unexpected crisis, it can take a lifetime. Annie Dillard acknowledges the painful process of changing our minds this way, "There are no events but thoughts and the heart's hard turning, the heart's slow learning where to love and whom."[1]

We find, as in the example of Christ, that leaders and teachers who target worldviews need a generous supply of courage mixed with gentleness. We also need art.

One of the primary roles of an artist is to enlighten us to the fact that we are seeing the world through glasses. Upon recognizing this, we are encouraged to do the hardest thing of all: take the glasses off and examine them. By making room for thoughtful conversation about previously held assumptions, art ultimately helps us adjust our lenses in order that we may be more fully aware and truthful. The experiential nature of art has the ability to subtly penetrate our consciousness and provoke us toward self-examination as individuals, churches, and societies. Good artists are usually aware of the exciting reflective potential inherent in their craft.

Many pastors find it easier and more practical in terms of growth and efficiency to reinforce the Western Evangelical worldview that predominantly walks through our doors. If we want to genuinely live into the way of Jesus, however, we must say something different. The only way we will change the worldview of our people is to plop ourselves down inside the hidden places where their belief and behavior are actually informed.

Considering the importance of good worldview, I've outlined the "shape" of three lenses that I've encountered both in myself and in the church throughout the years.

THE BIFURCATED LENS

A lens that views the world as either sacred or secular is what I call a bifurcated or split lens. A person with such a world-view would suggest that there are a *few* things that have eternal consequence; for many Evangelicals these are things associated with the church or preceded by the label "Christian." The other secular things simply don't matter in the grand perspective of eternity. They are inconveniences and distractions we have to endure, tolerate, and perhaps even avoid.

For example, far too many people in the church consider their vocation a "job"—an English slang term for a criminal activity—and endure it only in order to survive. The secular job puts food on the table and sends kids to college. Work is a necessary evil and heaven eternal play, says the person who views vocation in this way.

Entertainment seen through the bifurcated lens is largely in-substantial unless overtly labeled Christian entertainment with a Christian message.

The bifurcated lens is well exampled in the story of two Hollywood movies both released in 2004. Within a few months of each other, two rather heavy-handed films both dealing with evil and redemption were released to the general public. One was a film by Mel Gibson depicting the suffering and crucifixion of Jesus Christ and the other was a retelling of the 1994 Rwandan genocide.

Mel Gibson's *The Passion of the Christ* doesn't vary from the story we know well. *Hotel Rwanda,* on the other hand, tells a story of which many people in America, including the American church, are largely unaware. The contemporary story poses provocative questions about responsibility and morality.

Even though it is widely acknowledged among filmgoers and critics alike that *Hotel Rwanda* is significant (garnering three Academy Award nominations for acting and screenplay), the Christian community has largely ignored the film.

It is in no way an overstatement to suggest that the American church is largely responsible for *The Passion of the Christ*'s overwhelming opening weekend gross of $83 million. Meanwhile, *Hotel Rwanda*—the redemptive film that lacks an overtly Christian label—opened in fourteenth place with a weekend gross of $100 thousand.[2]

Adopting a new worldview begins with the practice of seeing God everywhere. God's redemptive story, in which broken things are continually in the process of being made whole, accounts for all of existence. The cross moves us toward the grand consummation of a promise: greater life than we can presently imagine. So we keep practicing imagination toward this end, recognizing the way things *ought* to be versus the way things currently *are,* the way they *can* be, and the way they someday *will* be. Everything has a place in this story.

If we engage the hard work of seeing the world as what Dallas Willard calls "a God-bathed world,"[3] then we develop the habit of discerning what is good and extracting truth from everything we encounter. Not everything is good, but all things are accounted for. Everything has a place in this grand, redemptive narrative. God is calling the church to live into his original mandate (Genesis 12) to be a people who bless rather than curse, and create rather than criticize. More employed by the gospel are the people who seek redemption for the world than those who attempt flight from it.

Art provides a wonderful training ground and opportunity to challenge the bifurcated lens. As we engage art forms we are afforded the opportunity to ask ourselves, is truth expressed? Where is God here? How does this speak to the narrative we are all part of?

What do you see?

As I leave movie theaters with my children I always ask, "What truth did you see?" For years they just looked at me with confusion. But one day after watching *Despicable Me,* my son furrowed his brow and said, "Well . . . even bad people have good in them."

We have the same conversations at our gallery on First Fridays.

When engaged intentionally, art can be amazingly formative to our worldview.

THE FRAGILE LENS

What do you see? Art provokes this question, and our answer is revealing.

The church's answer to what we see in art reveals that we are looking through a fragile lens. Consider a recent conversation I had. I was discussing with a friend a popular film that portrayed multidimensional characters wrestling with life's ultimate questions. This person's first and only words about the movie condemned a brief sex scene in the film. "I don't have to expose myself to that, Jon," she said. "You know those images are imprinted on our minds once we're exposed to them."

I was initially confused because I couldn't remember any sex scenes in the movie. Whatever was supposed to be permanently imprinted on my mind had somehow bypassed me.

After a short while of reflection I was able to remember what she was referring to—a non-gratuitous scene lasting three seconds. Three seconds out of a two-hour movie, and yet those three seconds were all she saw. My friend couldn't move into a conversation about anything redemptive in the film because, for her, the movie was three seconds long.

What do we see? She only saw sex. And though I assume her attempt to be discerning was genuine, it revealed something I know to be true of the larger church—a failure to perceive truth inside of narrative. Conversations like the one I had with my friend are telling. Art exposes and subverts our largely unconscious worldview, revealing its illusions. Unfortunately, many of us within the church are wearing this fragile lens. We simply can't take much unpleasantness or ambiguity. We are too easily frightened and almost always offended. Too often, the church assumes that fragility equates to purity.

People who are easily offended are usually the same people who crave safety. When in a protective mode, we tend to flee from anything potentially offensive. Faith communities form Christian ghettos and safe places largely protected from the surrounding world. For such communities art is a tricky issue. As we have discussed, art provokes, and fear can keep us from discerning good amid provocative ideas. We are frightened of offending people because offended people flee. In general, there's nothing less appealing to the mainstream church than offended, fleeing people.

Christians are famous for inventing their own brand of art, free of anything potentially offensive. Unfortunately, although our

Unfortunately, although our art doesn't offend, it too often fails to provoke.

art doesn't offend, it too often fails to provoke. This lack of provocation is regretful when you consider that a provoked people will demonstrate behavior opposite of flight. Provoked people, similar to those existing in tension, engage. A person who is roused and stimulated by something is usually motivated to get more involved. When the church refuses to see the whole picture, we not only lose our credibility as social commentators but also forfeit any possibility to effect social change.

One of the church's chief tasks is to help its people engage culture. In order to be a blessing to the world, however, the church must first be present. The lens we wear goes a long way in determining if we can deal with and ultimately change the culture around us. We have to quit glorifying fragility by subtly attributing virtues such as purity to a church body that is, in actuality, just afraid.

Because art is by nature provocative, it can prove invaluable in developing a worldview that welcomes tension and equips the church for redemptive works.

THE UNDERSIZED LENS

My daughter is nine years old. When I ask her what she thinks about a movie, book, or painting she generally gives one of two answers: "I like it" or "I don't like it." She recently figured out that if she *really* likes something she can say, "I love it." It can be challenging to move beyond an elementary comprehension when engaging art with children.

Her reaction, of course, is perfectly normal for a nine-year-old girl. In general, children haven't developed the ability to articulate thoughts and emotions. Ask them how they feel about art with no guided questions and you will more than likely hear opinions ranging from "good" to "bad."

I'm suggesting we live in a culture that doesn't operate with a maturity much beyond our children when it comes to processing and responding to art. Although we excel at getting things done and accomplishing tasks, we haven't trained ourselves to be contemplative. We're a thumbs-up/thumbs-down culture. Thumbs-up is quick and efficient, but it deprives us of the opportunity to ingest and contemplate, both of which are necessary for transformation.

We have to allow something to become part of us if it is going to affect us in any lasting and meaningful way. Think of our body's relationship with food: the ingestion process involves both consuming nutrients necessary for healthy growth and discarding useless and potentially harmful properties.

Of course in order to be healthy humans we have to ingest more than just food. We are consuming any number of stimuli in a given moment, and so Eugene Petersen says regarding Scripture, we need to "eat" this book![4] If we don't learn the practice and habit of critically ingesting our experiences, we run the risk of remaining stunted in our growth toward maturity.

Although it may sound superficial, one of the best ways to practice the discipline of ingestion is to stretch ourselves beyond "I like it" or "I don't like it" sentiments when engaging art. Not only should the church move beyond approving/disapproving metrics, but we ought to be distinguished by our ability to reflect meaningfully on all aspects of life. Art provides the necessary training ground for intentionality and thoughtfulness.

Not only this, but art also has the ability to penetrate and transform our imagination. Like food, however, good ingestion takes time. As a kid, does anyone else remember waiting thirty minutes after eating before being allowed back in the pool?

One of the primary reasons art is greatly underappreciated and marginalized in the church, and in culture at large, is due to the time constraints we impose on ourselves. To appreciate and allow for art takes time and focus, elements that are also necessary for spiritual formation.

As the church we have a responsibility to slow down and process truth and reality. Such a commitment, though countercultural, is important to our human flourishing. When as church leaders we demonstrate and teach ingestion, we affirm to our members that all of life is important and worth observation. We can't afford to be driven solely by results. Our humanity is at stake.

The world groans as it patiently waits for the church to adjust its lens.

- Why do you think people cling to their worldviews and are reluctant to question them?

- Give some examples of ways that our faith is shaped by the dominant culture (rather than the other way around).

- When have you experienced a bifurcated lens? How did you address it?

- How does art challenge a fragile lens? Why is this healthy?

- How is a thumbs-up/thumbs-down culture threatening to the church's overall vocation?

- What are some other possible "lens shapes"?

PICTURE US

"The church is the single, multiethnic family promised by the creator God to Abraham. It was brought into being through Israel's Messiah, Jesus; it was energized by God's Spirit; and it was called to bring the transformative news of God's rescuing justice to the whole creation."

—*N. T. Wright*

I wrestle with what the church is and what it's for (an intimidating thing to admit being a pastor and all). And so ecclesiology, the study of the church, has been of primary interest to me for quite some time. I've read a lot of ecclesiology. I've taught sermons on it. And I can tell you from firsthand experience that there are a number of thoughtful commentaries about the church and its purposes. A lot of good books. Many worthy discussions.

Where ecclesiology becomes interesting for me is the point at which it becomes integrated with practice. After all, practice and experience are central to our formation of thought.

After working for many years on church staffs and with various congregations, I can't help but identify one underlying assumption they all shared: a belief that they, the church, existed for growth. In fact, without exception, all of the churches in which I've ever worked measured their health numerically. In this way, my practiced ecclesiology led me to understand the church as something that exists only to proliferate. Like a plant absorbing sunlight to make food in order to gain more sunlight, I figured the church absorbs people to use those people to get more people. And right or wrong, when I saw a church mission statement that read, "we exist to make disciples who make disciples" (quite a common mission these days), I immediately thought, *What you really mean is you exist to make members who will make members.* As I mentioned above, years of ministry practices and experiences had greatly formed me in this thinking. I could talk ecclesiology all day, but in practice I had never experienced a church where the idea of self-sustained growth wasn't central, although often unspoken, to every program and every ministry.

I'm not interested in using this space to deconstruct church growth movements and attractional models of church. In fact, growth itself can be, if handled responsibly and thoughtfully, at least one decent barometer of church health. The issue at hand isn't church growth as much as it is our shared ecclesiology. Is it possible to develop a faithful ecclesiology in the shadow of our modern preoccupation with size and numbers? In other words, has a complete fixation with church growth simply replaced well lived-out ecclesiology?

My pursuit of an orthodox ecclesiology returned me to two tasks in which (I thought) I was already thoroughly indoctrinated—evangelism and discipleship. For now, a word about the former.

THE TASK OF EVANGELISM

Evangelism is a hugely consequential task to any ecclesiology worth its salt. Proclaiming Jesus, gently persuading people to consider a whole new way of being human and relating to God, is at the heart of our ecclesiological calling; on this we can all agree.

We intuitively recognize that the church must be about the business of evangelism, so much so that the term *evangelism* can be attached to almost any program or strategy in order to automatically justify its existence and cost. Certainly our passion for evangelism is not in question.

But our understanding of it may be.

I believe the modern obsession with church growth is directly related to an honest mistake—a mistake that's easy to make considering the culture we live in. The mistake is a reductionistic view of our holy task. The cultural disposition towards pragmatism and sentimentality convinces us that the more people we recruit to our agenda, the better. Bigger is better. Ask anyone. Better yet, don't ask, just look.

How do we evangelize? We bring people in. We herd them. We create programs that reach specific target groups. We cater to needs and we offer services. Anything. Anything to draw people. As long as people come and the project helps create the proverbial "scene," then it falls under the wide—and often theologically ambiguous—evangelical blanket.

As I alluded to earlier, when we moved our church to the Kansas City Arts District and began operating a gallery, it wasn't uncommon to hear statements such as, "Oh, I see. You're targeting the art community." The assumption was always that our gallery was created in order to get people—specific people—into the church. And who would argue this? Souls are at stake . . . aren't they?

To be sure, something is at stake, but I'm not sure it's souls. As counterintuitive as it may sound, I think evangelism is encumbered and even slightly threatened in its current marriage with measurable and quantifiable growth. I have to wonder if it's not a coincidence that our understanding of the church's primary task looks so similar to the Western culture's image of success.

THE TRANSFORMATIVE POWER OF BEAUTY

I haven't come to a resting place in my personal pursuit of a resonant ecclesiology. Perhaps I never will. One thing I feel confident of, however, is that it is right to hold evangelism in prominence. Sharing good news is consequential and deserving of our sweat, and I understand this even more so now that my understanding of evangelism has changed.

Rather than focusing our evangelism on drawing crowds in order to persuade (at best) or manipulate (at worst), what if we focused our efforts on the hard work of making the world a better place? What if evangelism became identified with the task of seeking, generating, and sustaining two essential Christian virtues—justice and beauty?

A lot has be said about the church's involvement with justice and beauty, and for purposes of this book I want to focus our attention on the latter. More specifically, I want to express the growing need for the church to consider as part of our evangelical task the discovering, uncovering, and creating of beauty.

The tendency is to view beauty and art as peripheral to the ecclesial conversation, and yet to do so is to tell a partial story about the work God is doing and will do in the world. N. T. Wright

Ugliness is an enemy of humanity and responsible for creating lives of hopelessness, defeat, and loss.

emphasizes that beauty is not only essential in conveying mean-ing, but that it is a "highway into the very center of reality."[1] The truth about reality, and more specifically God's redemptive real-ity, is not easily glimpsed or grasped because it's not yet here in full. However, beauty serves as a medium for truth. It tells us an important part of the story. Beauty begins to provide us hope amidst the ugliness of present circumstances and living condi-tions by reassuring people that "the present world is designed for something which has not happened yet."[2]

In an Evangelical culture that too often draws lines in the sand and takes unnecessarily rigid stances against trivial things, I am hesitant to ever label something as an "enemy." But I truly believe that ugliness is an enemy of humanity and responsible for creating lives of hopelessness, defeat, and loss. Wright calls ugliness one of the prominent features of the post-industrial West and laments its negative effect on human prosperity. "The shoulder-shrugging functionalism of postwar architecture, cou-pled with the passivity born of decades of television, has meant that for many people the world appears to offer little but bleak urban landscapes, on one hand, and tawdry entertainment on the other. And when people cease to be surrounded by beauty, they cease to hope. They internalize the message of their eyes and ears, the message that whispers that they are not worth very much, that they are in effect less than fully human."[3]

To be wrapped up in God's idea of beauty, then, is to assign a certain meaning to mankind. That the great, cosmic, redemptive battle is one in which beauty overtakes ugliness in all its various forms and expressions is proof of the value God places on each human life. In order to align ourselves with God's mission, the church must also become a community that promotes beauty and fights what is ugly, corrupt, and empty. We must be continually advocating and working toward all things beautiful—beautiful relationships, beautiful neighborhoods, and beautiful aesthetics.

A friend once confessed an intimate and moving story having to do with his pornography addiction. The story centered around a breakthrough moment which led to the end of his destructive habit. Here is what's striking, his transformation didn't begin in the local church. It began in an art shop. This is what he said:

> There was one shop in town–a mom-and-pop video store that I frequented weekly. It was out of the way and, therefore, safe; no one knew me there.
>
> I always parked a couple of blocks away and walked for anonymity's sake. One day I approached the store as usual and noticed a new business in the space next to the video store. It was an art shop. I ducked my head as I walked by not wanting to make eye contact with anyone, but I managed to glimpse the paintings in the window. I can't remember now what kind of paintings they were, but I do remember

rich colors everywhere. I slowed down and took notice of the work, and by the time I reached the video store my eyes had teared up. *What is going on with me?* I looked back at the paintings and then at the all too familiar adult video section. I couldn't put my finger on it at the time, but I was struck by the disparity between the two—real creativity and beauty as opposed to the ugliness that awaited me inside the video store.

This is when I realized my secret habit was limiting my own potential for creativity. It was keeping me from being everything I was meant to be. I didn't go through the door that day because I was unable. Not in light of the facts. I realized that if I was going to continue renting pornography then I would have to find another store . . . one that wasn't next to an art shop."

Beauty is consequential, pointing those who care to notice it toward a greater reality. I believe that this great and beautiful reality will win, resulting in a day when ugliness, in all its forms, will be eradicated.

But it will be a long and hard battle.

My ecclesiology tells me true and pure evangelism takes time. Beauty and justice aren't three step programs. And while beauty is fun to talk about, it's not easy to create—not even always easy to recognize. (Remember the Joshua Bell experiment at L'Enfant Plaza?)

Ugliness, on the other hand, is easy. If there's anything we learn about sin from its first appearance in Genesis, it's that it can be characterized by thoughtlessness. The grand feat of rejecting God looks like nothing more than biting into a piece of fruit.

THE TASK OF DISCIPLESHIP

If evangelism is *sharing* good and beautiful news, then it may be appropriate to say that discipleship is the process in which we thoughtfully conceive good and beautiful news. It may be appropriate to say, also, that a person conceiving the good news will be transformed by it, will become good news him- or herself. My friend and I joke that we always know a church's mission statement before reading it. They are all very similar in nature, revolving around the word *disciple* and the endeavor to "make disciples." Of course, no one can argue the validity of that mission—it's what Christ calls us to do! The hours of sweat, however, ought to be saved for fleshing out what the word "discipleship" actually means. In short, what does it look like to make a disciple? or to become a disciple? What picture comes into your imagination when you envision discipleship? A classroom? A family? Words are fine, but it's what we picture—and what picture we make—that carries the real weight. For instance, I've noticed discipleship pastors are often functionally small-group pastors. That means, for many of us, discipleship looks like weekly home meetings over curriculum and coffee. Is this an adequate picture of making disciples? Chatting over coffee and cakes? Is this the good news? Maybe in part.

The point is that the picture tells the story, and there is more to the story. We can say we are all about making disciples, but what we imagine that looking like in action determines what we do and don't do. What if a church, instead of words, presented pictures every Sunday to better communicate their mission statement? (Furthermore, what if that church eventually *became* a picture of their mission statement?) Certainly a picture might say much more about our churches and better inform our practices. Pictures might also more clearly communicate what we mean when we talk about discipleship making.

Of course words can be useful in painting pictures.

One of the reasons our church leadership chose the name Beggars Table is specifically because the words form a picture, and that picture helps shape imaginations toward who we want to be. It has proven both a helpful and a scary choice. People interpret pictures differently and, depending on the person, our name provokes a variety of responses—not all favorable and approving.

Some people say things like, "I love your church name. It really sums it all up." They picture a communion of broken people somehow gathered and fed despite their brokenness. Sometimes they go on further to say God is serving the food in their interpretation of the picture. I've heard others interpret it differently.

"Beggars? We're not beggars! As children of God we're glorious beings. It insults me to be called a beggar . . ."

Initially I felt the temptation to explain away our picture. Click here and let us clarify the good intentions behind our name. After growing weary with trying to explain, I now refrain: *Wait,* I tell myself. *Just let the picture work.*

How people interpret pictures reveals helpful insights into that person. It reveals particular bents of that person's faith and, perhaps most importantly, what he or she understands church to be. Chances are, the person who reacts negatively to a picture of dependent beggars communing around a table isn't going to like our church no matter how many wordy explanations we offer. Why not let the picture do its work and, in a sense, filter for us?

However a church pictures discipleship, allowing a picture to speak is much riskier than safely regurgitating the same generic phrases found in mission statements. Pictures reveal, filter, and ultimately provide meaning to what we actually do.

FAITHFUL IN ESSENCE

I confessed in an earlier chapter my love for stories. I admitted my deeply held secret that fiction and popular literature often stir my heart more than so much well-intentioned Christian literature. I believe this is primarily because most Christian literature is propositional in nature. As Smith says, "The cognitive and propositional is easily reduced and marginalized as just more 'blah-blah-blah' when our hearts and imaginations are captured by a more compelling picture of the good life."[4]

If we're not fundamentally informational beings, then the church needs to explore ways of freeing itself from predominantly informational mediums. Beggars Table has the same struggles as most churches addressing this paradigm shift. In fact, because our teaching is often dialectic in nature and involves questions and communal participation, our Sunday gathering is sometimes compared to a classroom (much to the chagrin of its leadership).

But we also increasingly incorporate elements designed to get us out of our heads. Communion is a weekly practice at our church, and we serve it in a way that requires people to leave their chairs, physically move their bodies, and walk forward to touch, smell, and taste the sacred elements. A common practice for Beggars Table during the Lenten season is to hang pictures around our gallery depicting the seven last words of Jesus on the cross. As part of our structured worship time, we often invite people to quietly walk around the room and spend time at each station reflecting and praying as they view the pictures. I've received some pretty powerful feedback around this practice.

To be human is to love. Throughout this text I have sought to add some thoughtful commentary around my community's experience with art as it has to do with making us more faithful in our love. In this way I have meant to engage, to some degree,

How might we be gotten to?

How are we transformed?

questions like: How might we be gotten to? How are we transformed?

Because people operate on an emotional, instinctual, and preconscious level, we are learning at Beggars Table to interact with faith on those levels that transcend the cerebral. Though we cannot comprehend the vast mysteries of God—which is not the point—we can allow God to comprehend us through art, story, and experience.

For this reason we are rehearsing, observing, performing, and reciting, with elements, liturgy, songs, and work, using eyes ears, mouths, and limbs. We want to encounter faith until sooner or later it begins to inhabit and embody us; until we are essentially —in essence—faithful.

We have already discussed the power of imagination and how our picture of the good life is responsible for shaping our love and ultimately our behavior. The good life isn't only for us. God gives us imagination in order that we may help others imagine. Or put another way, he blesses us in order that we may bless.

Father God, transform us into a picture of the good life. Make us into your kingdom so that the world may be blessed. Amen.

- What Scriptures have provided you with a compelling picture of the good life? Any unscriptural pictures? or stories?

- What does discipleship look like in your local congregation? What do you want it to look like?

- Why is it so important to engage our senses when it comes to worship? What are ways to go about making our services more corporeal?

- The title of this chapter is "Picture Us." What does it mean to you that God uses the church as a picture of his kingdom? Does his belief in the church change your opinion toward it? How so?

POSTSCRIPT: ART IS NOT (ALWAYS) SEXY

It's not unfashionable for the church to talk about the arts. Truth be told, there's a certain trendiness surrounding this whole conversation in Evangelical circles today.

That's all well and good, but we need to broaden the scope of what is actually at stake. A young hipster congregation doesn't necessarily qualify a church as artistic, neither does loud music or a lot of candles. The issue of artfulness is much deeper than that of worship *style.*

I don't want to dissuade you from the stylish, but instead draw your attention to the idea that there is a decidedly unsexy element involved in truly embracing the arts. Fleshing out some of the theology discussed here is not a quick pathway to popularity, rampant hype, and huge churches. There is a toll involved with being a misfit.

Without question there are a lot of congregations today that look and sound different than the conventional stereotype, but upon scratching the surface you often find the same culturally conditioned assumptions and worldviews at work. Bringing artists out from the margins and allowing them a prominent voice is like walking upstream. It's not easy.

Invite participation. Ask for creative and spontaneous contribution. Slow down. Be still. Allow for mystery. Ask questions. Minimize emotional manipulation but encourage emotion. Surround your congregation with art that doesn't have an overtly religious agenda. This kind of thing sometimes takes getting used to. Everyone comes to community with certain expectations, most of which are shaped by previous church experiences. Expectations are powerful influencers.

At its core, art isn't about appealing to anyone except the artist himself or herself. To get right down to it, it's kind of a selfish expression, in the best sense of the word. After years of trying to provide people with various rationales for planting a church, I finally became comfortable telling the truth: "I want to plant the church that I've always wanted. I want to bring to fruition what I desire in my own heart."

This is the artist's heart speaking: *I'm making what my heart desires and creating according to my innermost inclinations. I'm not hiding behind any agenda. I selfishly want this.*

One time a well-intentioned mentor squirmed when he heard me say this. He tried to correct me, "You mean you're doing what God wants."

My response, "Why do we assume the two have to be so different?"

I sometimes wonder if it's possible to genuinely reintegrate art and faith *and* appeal to the masses at the same time. As church leaders, we may very well face the same dilemma painters face when deciding not to follow in the footsteps of the widely disseminated Thomas Kinkade, in favor of following their peculiar leanings. We may be like those filmmakers who insist on making something completely original over and above the studio's

POSTSCRIPT: ART IS NOT (ALWAYS) SEXY

demand for commercial appeal. Or perhaps we are the authors who consider more than the best-seller lists. The choice to follow art, even to the margins, is ours.

Of course, there are wonderful examples of large churches that engage the arts very effectively. Sometimes artists find a niche with the popular imagination and become amazingly fashionable. Many times they don't. I'm certainly not saying that a church can't grow while fostering faith and the arts.

I'm just saying . . .

VIDEO TRANSCRIPTS: INTRO

Right now we're in the space that Beggars Table meets in. This is a loft in the Arts District of Kansas City—we call it the Crossroads. Specifically, right now is First Fridays. On the first Friday of each month, all the galleries in the Crossroads District open their doors and people come down in droves to walk through the galleries and engage the art.

Instead of [church] being that place that people walk by or drive by and point to saying, "there's the church," I'm more enticed by the idea of [church] being an activity or presence that people are engaged in without realizing until later. So, for example, on First Fridays you'll have people engaging the art here and completely unaware that they're participating in church. We're a felt presence—more than a visible entity shouting out, "We're a church! We're trying to reach you!"

When we first decided to move Beggars Table down here to the Crossroads, I remember meeting with a man that lived here and was involved with the neighborhood. He was a little bit of an older gentleman, but he took me around and walked me around to all the important places downtown; I remember him talking about all the people that we would need to reach. He had this long list of people we'd need to reach, and I remember that I started to feel nervous and anxious. I also started to just feel depressed. I remember at that time that, as passionate as I am about the church, I was not interested in reaching all those people. I even started to question how interested I was in reaching anyone. I realized that my vision for the church has more to do with being a felt presence in the neighborhood, and I was excited about the church being here and having a voice at the table—participating in the conversation.

Through years of conversation and mentoring with different people, we zeroed in on two words that mean a lot to us. Those are the words *seamless* and *responsible*. We actually use the words to help describe the kind of faith that we try to nurture. What we mean by seamless is that everything is God's. We try to break down that which divides the world into the sacred and the secular. Our conversation, rather than being, "What's sacred and what's secular?" tries to be about, "Where is brokenness and how can that brokenness be redeemed?" That leads into the second word: responsible. Responsible means a faith that's driven to act. We are creatures that are created with the ability to respond; we're response-able to God. We want to cultivate a faith that's not just a "believe-ism," but is something that helps to bring about redemption in all spheres of life. Seamlessness tells us it's not just church redemption, but that it's redemption for all spheres of life.

It's not uncommon to hear people question how you can be a church and an art gallery at the same time. That was a bifurcation people made that I was not ready for. You hear it often. People ask, "So do you have to take the art down in order to meet here? I mean, how can you worship in a place that has art?" They're probably wondering how we worship in a place that doesn't have overtly *Christian* art. What we're doing is trying to break down that bifurcation and marry faith to the arts again. That is one of the missions of Beggars Table.

VIDEO TRANSCRIPTS: CHAPTER 1

I like to look at humanity through the lens of the Imago Dei—the image of God. I think that we're all made with this ability to have critical thought and abstract thought. We're created with the ability to show grace and the ability to love. I believe that thinking lends itself to ideas, whereas feeling lends itself to impressions. Impressions are a lot more visceral; they encompass your sensations, your emotions, and your passions. So I think that if Descartes would have said, "I feel, therefore I am," he would have allowed Western civilization to somehow value feeling. I have always said that I think it would be a better-constructed sentence if it was "I think *and* I feel, therefore I am." We all live in tension with our thoughts and our feelings, and allowing ourselves to place value on our feelings is something that's a healthy motivator.

I remember one time I had a professor that said, "Art is a heroic obedience to the self-expression." If you took all of creation and applied that same sentence to God, saying that mankind was a heroic obedience to his self-expression and we are created in his image, it's only natural for us to go ahead and create as well. It's not always just beautiful pictures and portraits of light. Art is a way for people to express themselves and to be known. I think at the core of who God is, he wants to be known. I see in every artist that they're actually trying to somehow express themselves in a way that is more clear. Maybe it's not rational, maybe it's not linear, but it's a clear representation of who they are. I think just the act of creating is a Godly act in and of itself.

If you look at the sum of creation, you see a story. I think that if you were to look at it as a story—as a narrative—you would see a lot of mystery and enigma, but you'd also see a lot of magic and mysticism. If you were to paint creation as one single picture, you would give people a different way to access truth than simple dialogue or cognitive reasoning. So I think in a lot of ways art shows us glimpses of that truth and reveals certain things to us that cannot simply be told. In art, in music, in literature, and in film, artists' expressions of themselves and their perceptions of reality open up a door for someone else to gain access to a truth he or she couldn't necessarily receive through just a lecture or paper or discourse. We use ideas as ammunition when talking with other people, whereas art is more akin to feeling and more subjective. While we think that our thoughts are the way that we move forward, I think our feelings are what move us forward. Art reflects that movement. It is subjective. It's not something to which people can say, *Well, that's bad* or *That's good.* A theory or an idea or theology can be debated as being good or bad. But you cannot debate art. Art is an expression. I don't think it's the only way. I think people are bent on expressing themselves and their views with art. It's a different way of pointing to something other than themselves.

VIDEO TRANSCRIPTS: CHAPTER 2

Imagination is key in our church and even in our church name—Beggars Table. It's not an easily accessible name, but for most people it conjures up a response and an image (much more than, say, Second Pres). It's something that they're challenged by but invited into at the same time. I think that good imagination provides that tension. Like with a bow and arrow, too much tension and it breaks, but with the right amount you can really travel far and create something or do something over a long distance. I feel like that's what imagination does for us. Our culture doesn't do art on its own merits. I feel like we're very utilitarian and so we feel like art has to have an end game or purpose. We like to quantify it, and the easiest way to do that is financially.

I mean, the church has definitely become a check box for people of: *Okay, I've hit this status in my life. I need to do this. This is something I need to be involved in but not really allow to influence or change my life. I don't need it to give me a different lens or vision.*

I think a lot of that is based on the utilitarian aspect of it. We are good at giving you a program. We're good at telling you, "If you do this this and this, you're gonna be happy." We kind of sell a lie when the reality is, this is hard. Imagination is really hard. As we mature, we don't have the imagination of our childhood where it's just easy. It's a difficult thing. I feel like the church, because [art is] so difficult, doesn't really want a part of that conversation. It's a scary conversation. It's not black and white, there's a lot of gray. As we've seen in the history of the church, there's a lot of concern about the gray.

I think when the church, or anything for that matter, just bases its success on bottom line numbers, it tells just *part* of the story. A lot of times it's very common and popular to say the end justifies the means, and so we don't worry about the process or the *how*. The church falls into that trap a lot, and we end up mirroring the culture. Our divorce rates are the same. I would say teen pregnancy is probably the same. I would say that virginity, or loss of virginity, is the same. All of these things are the same because we don't have an intelligent or imaginative conversation about them.

I feel like we've struggled as a church to quantify how we are doing. For instance, growth. What's the role of growth? We have to mature, we have to grow as a church. Is growth numbers? You know, I can look around at our church and I can see the maturity in people's lives because they invite imagination and the opportunity for something different—the opportunity for beauty. It takes them on roads and paths of which somebody on the outside would say, "That's different. That's crazy."

That's what it should be.

This is a hard road, and to choose imagination is not an easy task.

We have the awesome privilege of changing our worship space every two months. So every two months we have a new artist up on the walls. And it does bring a different spirituality to the time. Just like the beauty of the architecture of gothic cathedrals, just like the stained glass windows, I mean, the art is our stained glass windows. So you end up focusing on one or two pieces while you are praying, while you are singing and praising, while you're listening and being challenged. There's this richness that the art can give and provide in that.

VIDEO TRANSCRIPTS: CHAPTER 3

If you grow up within a culture and you're given a single story and you know of no other things—the horizon, the barrier, the limit, the boundary—this is what defines. Why would you question it? Why would it even be alluring that there is something outside of that boundary? Because this is all you know. But it takes only one outsider or one experience, one pore, one crack in that boundary—I think in Jon's book he alludes to the hole in the wall to see the grandeur of this place that we was visiting—to say that it's not the end.

That *something more* is the invitation, the provocation, the craving that mystery presents. I think if everything is a given, then there's no space to move. It's absolutely a core relationship—where there is space to move, we are drawn into it. If there's no space to move, then it's not attractive.

It's true, we have tons of stuff. We have a lot of speed and a lot of connectivity, and yet the core of that question and why it's a trick—or a twist—is because having stuff hasn't necessarily increased our quality of life. It doesn't mean that our time hosts more value because we have more. That said, if we're empty, and we're talking about mystery, there is a chasm in us too. So it is into the chasm which the mystery moves. We too are the space. We are the opportunity for the possibilities. Because of our depravity or our own emptiness, there is now room for movement and growth. The deep provocations of actual value or actual meaning—as opposed to the false illusions of connectivity and relational values—are propped up with a scaffold.

As a painter myself, I love metaphor. One of the chief means that Christ used as an artist was metaphor. I think about Mary and the nature of the incarnation. What's beautiful about pregnancy is that we make room for the mystery—the unborn, the unknown, the life to come. We go through great pains to make room for said mystery, even when we have no specifics. We don't know how that life will walk out. But it's in that tension we find beauty, we find relationship, we find the basic groundwork for why we live and why we continue to do the things we do and value the things we value.

VIDEO TRANSCRIPTS: CHAPTER 4

I think what art does for us, one of the many things it can do for us, is to help us stay present to the integral congruence between medium and message. You know, it's like the classic Marshall McLuhan phrase the medium is the message. Artists know this, and I don't just mean artists like the kind of elite people who do paintings and photography and stuff. I'm also talking about people who live in a truly human, kind of creaturely way, and who are connected to the essence of what it is to be human. Art helps us stay present to that reality—to the congruence between the content that's trying to be delivered and the carrier (or sometimes the amplifier) of that content. It's only the rest of us that forget this once in a while. So, for example, I'm a pastor; I get emails once in a while from people in my congregation. If someone sends me an email with a list of supplies they need for something they're doing, that's fine; it's a rather impersonal thing to communicate using a rather impersonal, detached means. But if someone responds with a lengthy heartfelt email in response to something I've said, I often don't know if they're thoughtfully engaging me or angrily critiquing me. The medium limits what can be expressed because it's not human. It's disconnected. Somebody once said, "To a hammer, the whole world is a nail." I think for someone with an email account, the whole community is a list of contacts. We cease to be human beings. So art reminds us of our humanity; good art *always* reminds us of our humanity. The medium is always congruent with the message. You can't draw a line between them. If at times those things are ever separate, it's done intentionally to be sort of ironic.

Any medium—and by medium, I mean the thing we use to carry and sometimes amplify the message—has its limitations. If I'm going to come and speak to the church via video, and I'm Meryl Streep, then I'm going to be pretty confident that I can get across something that's very human and moving. But I'm not Meryl Streep, so I'm very nervous about having a mediated presence and not being with people. Mediums affect everything: the form, and the way the tone of the music and the key of the music carry the lyric of what's being proclaimed. In fact, I'm probably understating it. People like Marshall McLuhan would say (and I'll butcher this quote) that the content, or what we could call the message, has about as much affect on the recipient of that message as the stenciling on the casing of an atomic bomb. Right? It hardly matters what you write on the side—the medium is the message. You get the message when the bomb is delivered.

So when I stand in front of you as a human being and we're talking, there's something happening here that can't happen via video, that can't happen even over a phone call. There are some things that just require life on life, because I need to be able to feel you and you've got to be able to feel me. You can't do that on email unless you write with the precision of Dostoevsky or something. We're limited by the methods and the mediums that we choose.

All that artists are doing is reflecting the humanity that the rest of us carry around, right? So we go into other vocations and we forget that we're actually all artists—that we actually all know this stuff already. We know that the message and the medium are the same thing; they're so integral. And we build systems and methods and forms that sort of betray the fact that we're created in this integral way. We exist and we sort of play along [to those lesser systems]. But then you walk into a gallery like this—and there's a reason all these people come from the city to be here, right?—it's because you stand before one of these photographs or paintings and you start to get it again. *Oh! This isn't just a message and a medium. This is making me feel something . . . making me feel alive.*

Maybe [art is] intimidating. Maybe there's a reason we've kind of bifurcated the whole thing and we try to hold it apart. Maybe it's dangerous. Maybe it calls us back into something that's primal, something that we're not all that comfortable with because it's messy and it has to be constantly negotiated. Negotiation requires human on human contact. That's a lot harder to do.

VIDEO TRANSCRIPTS: CHAPTER 5

Worldview is how information comes in, how you digest it, and how you act based on what you perceive is happening around you. I think what we do is we put worldview in a box; for instance, you say, "This profession is the best way to make a living." That's your worldview. That's your opinion. That's what you live into, and your life revolves around the fact that what you do, your said job, is the best job out there.

In the church context, the bifurcated lens is a really easy split. There are things that God cares about and things that God doesn't care about. Those are called *sacred* and *secular*. So if it has to do with your faith or spreading the gospel or helping the needy or making other people Christians or making disciples, using that type of terminology, that is sacred. Secular would be where you shop, where you live, the clothes you buy, and where you send your kids to school. None of that stuff "matters" because it's not the end result of either getting yourself to heaven or getting somebody else to heaven.

When we put God so far away from the things that we do every day, in a time of crisis or in times of big decisions we're like, *God where are you? You're so far away. I feel so lonely. I feel so sad.* This is because we haven't taken the time to practice seeing God in the mundane, everyday, ordinary parts of our beautiful lives. We just haven't focused our attention.

The fragile lens is, *I'm not going to look at something because it offends me or it scares me or I just believe it's wrong so I'm not going to go there at all.* The fragile lens is the one that says, *I won't go to an R-Rated movie because it's R.* It's fine to not go to an R-rated movie, but if you see one, what was good? What was bad? What was redemptive? What wasn't? The person with a fragile lens can't have that conversation because he or she won't engage.

I think the fragile lens keeps us from engaging reality. Life is messy. Life is ugly. Life is hard. New Christians, or people who are coming to faith, they don't have the experience to know that when you become a Christian, life doesn't just get better. We sell them this bill that says as soon as you believe, Jesus is going to come into your life and it's going to make everything better. In six months when it doesn't, they feel let down. With a fragile lens we tell people subconsciously that being a Christian is really easy and that if it's not easy then they're just not believing hard enough. It's just tragic because people have so many different phases of life and so many phases of experience that we don't let play out. [We don't let people] live with the support of Christian community alongside of them.

I think the thumbs up/thumbs down approach to the question, "Do you like this piece or do you not like this piece?" is appropriate if you're planning on buying it. But sometimes when you go to an art gallery the purpose really isn't for you to buy something, it's for you to feel something. It's for you to look at something. It's for you to appreciate a new process. It's for you to understand what the artist is trying to say without using words.

The best times are when I can actually talk to the artist about what they did. I might not like the piece any more than I did after my first reaction to it, but I can appreciate it a lot more and I can respect what they were trying to say. I can evaluate how well they communicated their idea to me or not.

I think there's nothing scarier than having your worldview shifted or changed or stretched because the God you thought you knew and the faith you had now looks different. Sometimes I wish that I just kind of discovered Christ later in life so I didn't have to have such a massive worldview change. Or, I take that back, I would want something more defined like, *This is when it happened* or *This is when I started to change.* I feel like there are so many emotions involved with broadening your worldview; it's sadness and regret, and then it's just joy and *Wow! I can see God everywhere and I can appreciate what was here without anger or bitterness. I can appreciate my platform but I can see further now!* It's very exciting but I would say it takes years and I think worldviews are constantly evolving just the way that our faith, over our lifetime, looks so different. Just in my personal challenges it was different being single, it was different being married, it's different having kids, it's different being a landlord. Whatever my responsibilities are and whatever my life phase is, my faith has to grow with me or it will die.

VIDEO TRANSCRIPTS: CHAPTER 6

I don't want to undervalue the significance of words because words are important. Words can help paint pictures, and I do think that we all kind of operate fundamentally on the picture level. Whether we're aware of it or not we tend to envision or picture the things that are important to us. That's what motivates us more often than not.

One of the big things you do when you start your own church is you choose a name. It's like when you have a child and one of the big things you do is choose a name for your child. It always feels a little awkward because you feel like you're kind of pigeonholing your child. Same with your church. I remember there were a lot of initiatives to create a church name that revolved around a certain doctrine— a theological doctrine. We could have called our church *Grace* or *Christ's Community* or something like this. But those always rang hollow to me. I always wanted the name of this church to be something that would be more provocative and capture people's imagination. Beggars Table just happened to be a phrase that I stumbled upon and that I really loved. I realize now that one of the reasons I loved it was because it painted a picture. It was a picture that was not definitive. It wasn't telling people what to think about our church. It was allowing people to come up with their own ideas. Now, I've got some strong opinions about what Beggars Table alludes to and means, and why it's a healthy picture for a church community. But I like the idea of just putting it out there and letting people converse and dialogue amongst themselves about what it means. *Why is this church named this?*

Having a name like Beggars Table is very risky because people interpret that picture differently. It speaks in different ways to different people. Like I said in the book, how people interpret pictures reveals a lot about who they are and where they are in their journey. Now, obviously we want to be a church that's open to everyone who wants to come here. Everybody is welcome as long as they're willing to buy into who we are, but the picture that our name paints acts as sort of a filter. The people that react negatively to it expose a little bit of who they are. With that exposure they can either make the decision to go somewhere else, or to come here and engage and work through it.

The church is the visible image of God. We're the body of Jesus Christ, so the way that we look matters and it matters significantly. It's of primary importance for every church body, every pastor, and every church leader to pause, and to consider what their church looks like—what picture they are painting. When we gather, we're painting a picture whether we realize it or not. When we engage in any activity, we're painting a picture of Jesus Christ. It's a picture of who Christ is and that picture is important to the world. It speaks boldly and it speaks loudly. So the most important questions we can ask ourselves are: Who are we? What kind of picture are we painting of the kingdom of God? What does the kingdom look like, not just right now, but what it will look like someday? How do we embody that?

I think that, to a great degree, our picture of the church has to be held loosely. It's continually evolving, and not just at Beggars Table. I think that all churches need to let their church picture evolve because we are constantly learning about ourselves, learning about God, and learning about what it is that we want to be and how we embody the kingdom. So I think one of the dangers is to take a mission statement and write it in stone, not allowing ourselves to change as we grow. As God reveals more of who he is to us, we want our churches and the picture that we paint to grow.

NOTES

CHAPTER 1

1. James K. A. Smith, *Desiring the Kingdom: Worship, Worldview and Cultural Formation* (Grand Rapids, MI: Baker Publishing Group 2009), 44.

2. Ibid.

3. David Brooks, Introduction to *The Social Animal* (New York: Random House, 2011).

4. Stanley Hauerwas, "A Story-Formed Community: Reflections on *Watership Down*," in *The Hauerwas Reader*, ed. John Berkman and Michael Cartwright (Durham, NC: Duke University Press), 171-99.

CHAPTER 2

1. C. S. Lewis, "Bluspels and Flalansferes: A Semantic Nightmare" in *Selected Literary Essays* (Cambridge: Cambridge University Press, 1969), 251.

2. Robert Trexler, ed., "Signs and C. S. Lewis: The Meaning of Meaning, How Hobbits are Real, and the Value of Film" (New York: New York C. S. Lewis Society, 2005).

3. Makoto Fujimura, "Refractions 32: Emanuel's Heartbeat," July 17, 2009, http://www.makotofujimura.com/writings/refractions-32-emanuels-heartbeat/.

4. Ibid.

CHAPTER 3

1. Anne Lamott, *Plan B: Further Thoughts on Faith* (New York: the Penguin Group, 2005).

2. Michael Polanyi, "The Stability of Beliefs," *British Journal for the Philosophy of Science* 3, no. 11 (1952), 217-32.

3. Gene Weingarten, "Pearls Before Breakfast," *Washington Post*, April 8, 2007.

4. Makoto Fujimura, "Refractions 32: Emanuel's Heartbeat," July 17, 2009, http://www.makotofujimura.com/writings/refractions-32-emanuels-heartbeat/.

CHAPTER 4

1. Philip Sheldrake, *Spaces for the Sacred: Place, Memory, and Identity* (Baltimore MD: The John Hopkins University Press 2001), 60.

2. Ibid.

3. N. T. Wright, *Surprised By Hope: Rethinking Heaven, the Resurrection, and the Mission of the Church* (New York: HarperCollins, 2008), 231.

CHAPTER 5

1. Annie Dillard, *Holy the Firm* (New York: Harper & Row, 1977).

2. Box Office Mojo, "2004 Domestic Grosses," http://www.boxofficemojo.com/yearly/chart/?yr=2004.

3. Dallas Willard, *The Divine Conspiracy: Rediscovering Our Hidden Life in God* (New York: HarperCollins, 1998), 61-95.

4. Eugene Peterson, *Eat This Book: A Conversation in the Art of Spiritual Reading* (Grand Rapids, MI: Wm. B. Eerdmans Publishing Co., 2006).

CHAPTER 6

1. N. T. Wright, *Simply Christian: Why Christianity Makes Sense* (New York, NY: Harper Collins Publishers, 2006), 200.

2. Ibid.

3. N. T. Wright, *Surprised by Hope: Rethinking Heaven, the Resurrection, and the Mission of the Church* (New York: HarperCollins Publishers, 2008), 231.

4. James K. A. Smith, *Desiring the Kingdom: Worship, Worldview, and Cultural Formation* (Grand Rapids, MI: Baker Publishing Group, 2009), 54.